IQRA'S NOTE

As-Salamu 'Alaikum!

This book, *We Are Muslims,* has been written for First Grade children as part of **IQRA's** comprehensive and systematic program of Islamic Studies; a project that has been designed to be an integrated educational system facilitating the teaching of religious knowledge from a cross-curricular perspective.

We are Muslims (and its accompanying workbook) is part of IQRA's latest effort to revise and update its many publications. It has been written in a language comprehendible to elementary-level readers. We truly believe that children will be able to grasp all the concepts introduced in each lesson and adopt Islamic teachings into their everyday life.

We are Muslims introduces children to the basic elements of Islamic belief as well as the central rituals known as the Five Pillars of Islam. Students are also introduced to the concepts of Halal and Haram as well as the virtue of patience.

It is recommended that the teachers use the accompanying workbook along with the textbook during class time. The workbook has been designed to provide pupils with important exercises in comprehension and to aid in the development of critical thinking skills.

We invite you to join hands with IQRA' in our efforts to provide quality educational material. Please send us your comments and suggestions. It will be only through our cooperation and interaction that we will be able to build a viable and professional program of education for the coming generations, *Inshallah!*

Chief Editors
May, 2005

D1225735

CONTENT INDEX

CONTENT INDEX

ABOUT THE BOOK

TUNE IN
Verses of the Qur'an/ Hadith/ Poems and simple questions are presented to draw the reader's attention to the theme of the lesson.

Think About It
Graphic representations are used to teach critical thinking skills

We Have Learned
Main ideas of the lesson are summarized here to help the students recapitulate the themes.

Do You Know These Words?
New vocabulary words used in the lesson are introduced.

Link to Workbook
Indicates the corresponding activities in the workbook

WE ARE MUSLIMS

TUNE IN

Let us sing together:

"Allah made my family and
Allah made me,
Allah made my teachers and
Allah made me,
Allah made my friends and
Allah made me,
I am a Muslim and Allah made
me."

Let us find out what makes us
Muslims.

We are Muslims.
We say, "Allah is the only God."
We say, "Muhammad is the Messenger of Allah".

This is the *Shahadah.*

We believe in the Angels of Allah.

We believe in the Books of Allah.

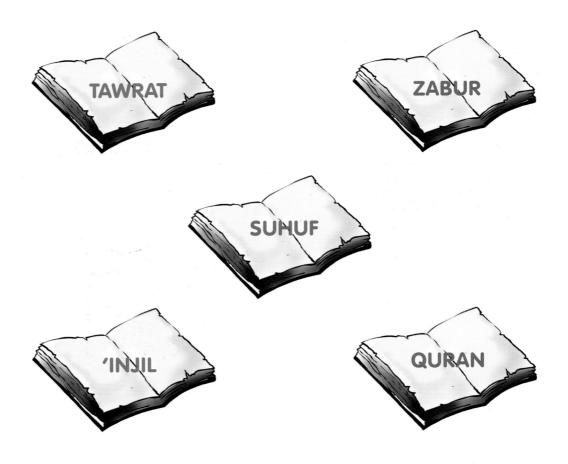

LESSON 1: WE ARE MUSLIMS

We believe in the Prophets of Allah.

We believe in the *Akhirah*.

We pray to Allah ﷻ.

We fast for Allah ﷻ.

We share for Allah ﷻ.

We go to *Hajj* for Allah ﷻ.

We say, "There is no God but Allah, and Muhammad is the Messenger of Allah."

La ilaha il Lallahu Muhammadur Rasulullah"

WE HAVE LEARNED

- **We believe that Allah ﷻ is the only God.**
- **Muhammad ﷺ is the last Prophet of Allah ﷻ.**
- **We pray only to Allah ﷻ.**
- **We fast and share for Allah ﷻ.**
- **We go to *Hajj* for Him .**

DO YOU KNOW THESE WORDS?

- **Muslim, believe, Prophet, Angel, *Hajj***

Link to Workbook Lesson 1

LESSON 1: WE ARE MUSLIMS

WE SAY GOOD WORDS

TUNE IN

Let us sing this song:

"When we meet a Muslim we say *Salam.*
As-Salamu 'Alaikum.
Wa-'alaikum As-Salam"

How many times a day do you say *Salam*?

Muslims use good words.
We thank Allah ﷻ.
We say *"Alhamdu Lillah."*
We say, "All Praise is for Allah ﷻ."

اَلْحَمْدُ اللَّهِ

We meet other Muslims.
We say *"As-Salamu 'Alaikum."*
We say "Peace be upon you."

We say, *"Bismillah ir-Rahman ir-Rahim"* when we begin something.

It means we begin, "In the Name of Allah ﷻ."

Muslims think of Allah ﷻ all the time.

We always ask for His help.

May Allah ﷻ help us to think of Him and say good words.

WE HAVE LEARNED

☾ **Muslims always say good words.**
☾ **We think of Allah ﷻ all the time.**
☾ **We say "As-Salamu 'Alaikum".**

DO YOU KNOW THESE WORDS?

☾ **Peace, *Alhamdu Lillah*, think, help**

Link to Workbook Lesson 2

LESSON 2: WE SAY GOOD WORDS

WE HAVE GOOD NAMES

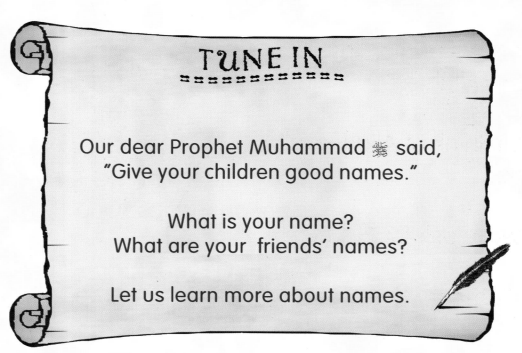

TUNE IN

Our dear Prophet Muhammad ﷺ said,
"Give your children good names."

What is your name?
What are your friends' names?

Let us learn more about names.

Muslims have good names.

My name is *Basma*.
Basma means, "Smiling".

My name is *Abdur Rahman*.
It means the "servant of
the Most Merciful".

Our mother is *Zahra*.
Zahra means "Rose".

Our father's name is *Hasan*.
Hasan means "Good".

What is your name?
What does it mean?

WE HAVE LEARNED

☾ **A Muslim should have a good name.**
☾ **We should know the meaning of our names.**

DO YOU KNOW THESE WORDS?

☾ **Children, *Basma*, *Hasan*, *Zahra*, *Abdur Rahman***

Link to Workbook Lesson 3

LESSON 3: WE HAVE GOOD NAMES

WE WEAR GOOD CLOTHES

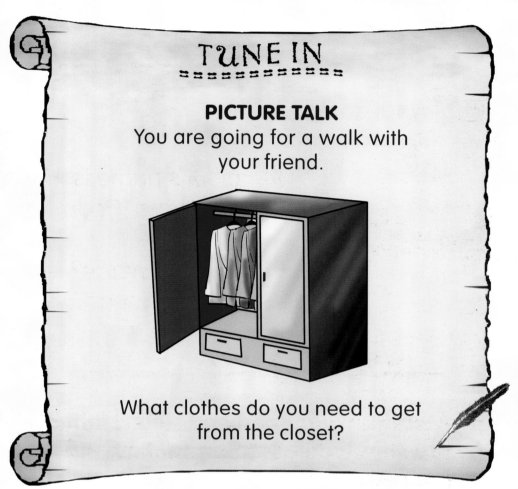

TUNE IN

PICTURE TALK
You are going for a walk with your friend.

What clothes do you need to get from the closet?

Muslims like good clothes. We like clean clothes.

Muslims wear all kinds of clothes.

Some wear bright clothes.
Some wear dark clothes.

Some Muslims wear warm clothes.
Some Muslims wear cool clothes.

What do you like to wear?

WE HAVE LEARNED

- ☾ **Muslims wear good and clean clothes.**
- ☾ **Muslims wear clothes that cover their bodies well.**
- ☾ **Muslims wear different kinds of clothes.**

DO YOU KNOW THESE WORDS?

- ☾ **Clean, good, clothes, wear**

Link to Workbook Lesson 4

LESSON 4: WE WEAR GOOD CLOTHES

THINK ABOUT IT

Muslims wear different kind of clothes to go to different places.

Muslims wear different kind of clothes at different times.

Read and name the different clothes we use below.

1. We wear uniform  when we go to school but

   we wear _____  when we go to bed.

2. A rain coat is used on a rainy day

   as _____  is used on a
   cold day.

LESSON 4: WE WEAR GOOD CLOTHES

WE ARE GOOD PEOPLE

Our Prophet ﷺ said,
"Be kind and merciful to everyone."

We do what our Prophet ﷺ wants us to do.

Let us find out.

Muslims do good things.
We are kind to people.
We are kind to animals.

We share with others.
We help every one.

We take care of our families.

We do not fight.
We do not get angry.
Allah ﷻ tells us to be good.

WE HAVE LEARNED

☾ **Muslims are good people.**
☾ **We are kind to every one.**
☾ **We do not fight with anyone.**

DO YOU KNOW THESE WORDS?

☾ **Kind, care, good, fight**

Link to Workbook Lesson 5

ALLAH ﷻ IS ONE

TUNE IN

Let us sing this song!
Allah ﷻ is Great: Allah ﷻ is One
He has no partner; daughter or son
In Him we believe; To Him we will give
Our love and our thanks,
For the things we receive.

Let us learn more about Allah ﷻ.

We are Muslims.

We say *Subhanahu wa Ta'ala* (ﷻ) when we say Allah.
It means the Most Glorified.

We believe that Allah ﷻ is ONE.

اَلْأَحَد

Allah ﷻ is *Al-Ahad*.
Al-Ahad means "The One".

We believe that there is no god but Allah ﷻ
Muhammad ﷺ is the Prophet of Allah ﷻ.
This is the *Shahadah*.

Muhammad ﷺ gave the message of Allah ﷻ to us.
We ask Allah ﷻ to bless Muhammad ﷺ.
When we say the name of Muhammad ﷺ,
we say "Sal Lallahu 'alaihi Wa Sallam" (ﷺ).
It means that the peace and blessings of Allah ﷻ be upon
him ﷺ .

Sal Lallahu 'alaihi Wa Sallam

WE HAVE LEARNED

☾ *Al-Ahad* means "The One".
☾ *Shahadah* means saying "There is no God but Allah and Muhammad is the Messenger of Allah."

DO YOU KNOW THESE WORDS?

☾ *Al-Ahad, Messenger, Shahadah*

Link to Workbook Lesson 6

LESSON 6: ALLAH ﷻ IS ONE

ALLAH ﷻ IS THE CREATOR

TUNE IN

PICTURE TALK

Can you tell us who made all of these?

Allah ﷻ made everything.
Allah ﷻ is the Creator, *Al-Khaliq.*

اَلْخَالِقِ

Allah ﷻ made us.
He made our mothers.
He made our fathers.

He made our families.
He made every one.

Allah ﷻ made the green forest.

LESSON 7: ALLAH ﷻ IS THE CREATOR

He made the animals in the forest.
He made the tall giraffe, the
small mouse and the
brave lion.

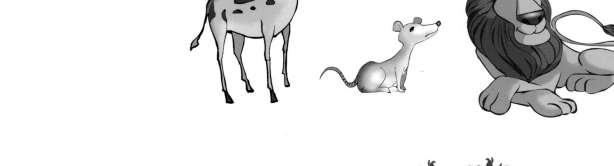

Allah ﷻ made the sea.
Allah ﷻ made the living
things in the sea.

Allah ﷻ made the
seahorse, the small fish,
the big blue whale.

LESSON 7: ALLAH ﷻ IS THE CREATOR

He made all the birds. He made the parrots, the peacock and the owl.

اَلْخَالِقِ

Who is *Al-Khaliq*, the Creator? Only Allah ﷾!

WE HAVE LEARNED

☾ Allah ﷾ is *Al-Khaliq*, the Creator.
☾ He made every one and every thing.

DO YOU KNOW THESE WORDS?

☾ *Al-Khaliq*, creator, sea, forest

Link to Workbook Lesson 7

LESSON 7: ALLAH ﷾ IS THE CREATOR

THINK ABOUT IT

Allah ﷻ is **Al-Khaliq.**

Allah ﷻ made many groups of things.

Write some of their names in each group.

Animals Living on Land

1. _____
2. _____

Animals Living in Water

1. _____
2. _____

Allah ﷻ has made all these

Animals Living on Land and in Water

1. _____
2. _____

LESSON 7: ALLAH ﷻ IS THE CREATOR

Allah ﷻ made many animals.

There are animals which live on farms.
There are animals that live in the forest.

Let us find out how they are alike and different in the chart below.

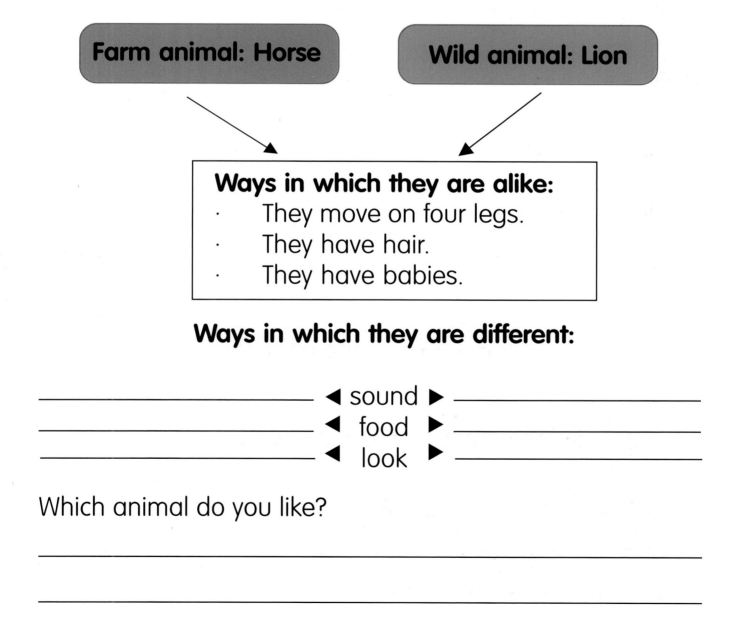

Farm animal: Horse

Wild animal: Lion

Ways in which they are alike:
·   They move on four legs.
·   They have hair.
·   They have babies.

Ways in which they are different:

_____ ◀ sound ▶ _____

_____ ◀ food ▶ _____

_____ ◀ look ▶ _____

Which animal do you like?

_____

_____

LESSON 7: ALLAH ﷻ IS THE CREATOR

ALLAH ﷻ IS ALL POWERFUL: AL-QAWI

TUNE IN

Be Thankful!
Allah ﷻ has done many favors to us.
Let us always thank Him and say
"Alhamdu Lillah".

اَلْحَمْدُ اللّٰه

Can you count His favors?

Allah ﷻ takes care of us. Allah ﷻ made us all. Allah ﷻ made our families. He takes care of us all. He takes care of our families.

Allah ﷻ makes the sun rise.
The sun gives us light.
It gives us heat.
Only Allah ﷻ can make the sun rise.
Allah ﷻ is All Powerful, *Al-Qawi*.

He makes the clouds in the sky.

We get rain from the clouds.
We get water from the rain.
We need water.

Only Allah ﷻ can give us water.
He is All Powerful, *Al-Qawi.*

LESSON 8: ALLAH ﷻ IS ALL POWERFUL: AL-QAWI

The Qur'an reminds us of the many favors of Allah ﷻ.

$$\text{وَجَعَلَ لَكُمُ ٱلسَّمْعَ وَٱلْأَبْصَٰرَ}$$

$$\text{وَٱلْأَفْـِٔدَةَ...}$$

*"And He has created for you ears, and eyes
and hearts..."*
(An-Nahl: 78)

Let us do what Allah ﷻ wants us to do.
Let us read the Qur'an.

WE HAVE LEARNED

- ☾ **Allah ﷻ is the All Powerful.**
- ☾ **He is *Al-Qawi*.**
- ☾ **We should do what Allah ﷻ tells us to do.**

DO YOU KNOW THESE WORDS?

- ☾ ***Al-Qawi*, powerful, sun, clouds, sky, rain,**

Link to
Workbook
Lesson 8

LESSON 8: ALLAH ﷻ IS ALL POWERFUL: *AL-QAWI*

ALLAH ﷻ IS KIND AND MERCIFUL

TUNE IN

Before we begin anything, we say,

بِسْمِ اللَّهِ الرَّحْمَنِ الرَّحِيمِ

"Bismillah ir- Rahman ir- Rahim"
In the name of Allah,
Most Kind, Most Merciful

Allah ﷻ loves us.

He is Kind. He is *Ar-Rahman*.
He is Merciful. He is *Ar-Rahim*.

He has given us our families.
We love our families.

We love our friends.
We love our neighbours.
We go to school with our friends.

He gives us food.
He gives us water.
Food and water help
us grow.

He has made the beautiful world.
We should take care of our world.
We should thank Allah ﷻ and say *"Alhamdu Lillah"*.

WE HAVE LEARNED

☾ **Allah** ﷻ **takes care of us.**
☾ **Allah** ﷻ **is Kind and Merciful.**
☾ **We should thank Allah** ﷻ **for everything.**

DO YOU KNOW THESE WORDS?

☾ **Merciful, kind, families, neighbors, world.**

Link to Workbook Lesson 9

WE LEARN FROM ALLAH'S ﷻ PROPHETS

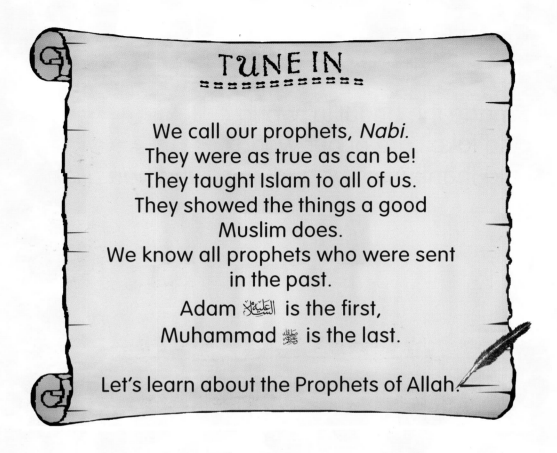

TUNE IN

We call our prophets, *Nabi.*
They were as true as can be!
They taught Islam to all of us.
They showed the things a good
Muslim does.
We know all prophets who were sent
in the past.
Adam عليه السلام is the first,
Muhammad ﷺ is the last.

Let's learn about the Prophets of Allah.

Allah ﷻ has sent many prophets.
He has sent them to all people.

The first prophet was Prophet Adam عليه السلام.
The last Prophet was Muhammad ﷺ.

ADAM عليه السلام ← → **MUHAMMAD** ﷺ

The Prophets told us that,

There is no god but Allah ﷻ.
We pray only to Allah ﷻ.
We ask Allah ﷻ for help.
All of us are brothers and sisters.

We are all children of Adam عليه السلام and Hawwa رضي الله عنه.

WE HAVE LEARNED

- ☾ **We believe in all the Prophets of Allah ﷻ.**
- ☾ **The first prophet was Adam عليه السلام.**
- ☾ **The last Prophet was Muhammad ﷺ.**

DO YOU KNOW THESE WORDS?

- ☾ **Help, first, last, children, take care**

Link to Workbook Lesson 10

THE BOOKS OF ALLAH

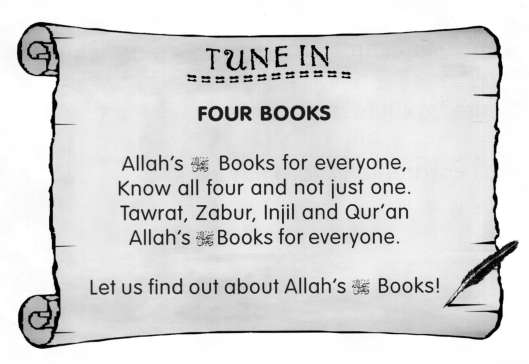

TUNE IN

FOUR BOOKS

Allah's Books for everyone,
Know all four and not just one.
Tawrat, Zabur, Injil and Qur'an
Allah's Books for everyone.

Let us find out about Allah's Books!

Allah told His Prophets to teach us.
Allah gave Books to some of His Prophets.

Allah asked Angel Jibril to recite the
Qur'an to Muhammad.

The Qur'an is the last Book of Allah.
Allah sent the Quran in Arabic language.

Allah ﷻ gave Zabur to Prophet Dawood السلام عليه.
Allah ﷻ gave Tawrat to Prophet Musa السلام عليه.
Allah ﷻ gave Injil to Prophet Isa السلام عليه.
Allah ﷻ gave Qur'an to Prophet Muhammad ﷺ.

In His Books, Allah ﷻ told us to pray to Him alone.
He told us to tell the truth.
He told us to share and help others.

LESSON 11: THE BOOKS OF ALLAH ﷻ

Allah  told us to respect our parents.

Allah told us to read and to think.

WE HAVE LEARNED

- ☾ **We believe in all the Books of Allah.**
- ☾ **The Qur'an is the last Book of Allah.**

DO YOU KNOW THESE WORDS?

- ☾ **Share, truth, help, respect, Jibril**

Link to Workbook Lesson 11

THINK ABOUT IT

Let us read and think!

We read storybooks.
We read Allah's Book, the Qur'an.
Let us find out about these two books

How are they alike?

Qu'ran	. We read about people. . They have beautiful covers. . The have writing.	Story Book

How are they different?

Arabic	**Language**	Many languages
Allah's teachings	**Content**	Make Believe

Both help us know about things. The Qur'an helps us know Allah's teachings. We are rewarded for reading the Qur'an.

THE ANGELS OF ALLAH ﷻ

TUNE IN

اقْرَأْ بِٱسْمِ رَبِّكَ ٱلَّذِى

"Read in the name of your Lord -"

Do you know who said these words to Prophet Muhammad ﷺ in the cave of Hira?

Let us find out!

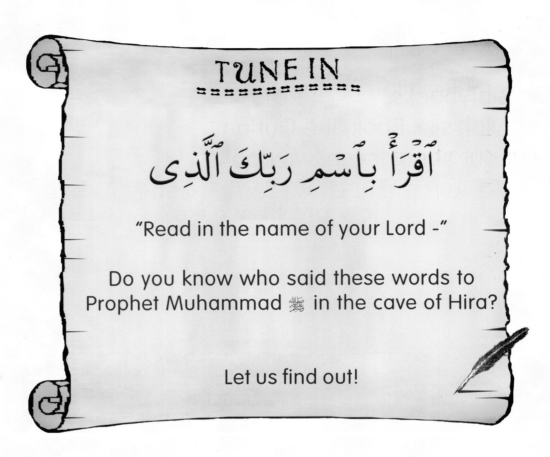

Allah ﷻ created Angels.
Angels are made of light.

Angels are good.
Angels are helpful.
Angels pray to Allah ﷻ
all the time.

Allah ﷻ created many Angels.

They make Allah ﷻ happy.
Let us make Allah ﷻ happy too!
Let us also be helpful to others.
Let us also be good.
Let us also remember to pray to Allah ﷻ.

WE HAVE LEARNED

☾ **Allah ﷻ made many Angels.**
☾ **Angels are made of light.**
☾ **Angels do what Allah ﷻ wants them to do.**

DO YOU KNOW THESE WORDS?

☾ **Create, happy, want, Angels, light**

Link to Workbook Lesson 12

LESSON 12: THE ANGELS OF ALLAH ﷻ

THE LAST DAY AND THE NEXT LIFE

TUNE IN

يَوْمَ يَكُونُ ٱلنَّاسُ كَٱلْفَرَاشِ ٱلْمَبْثُوثِ ٤

وَتَكُونُ ٱلْجِبَالُ كَٱلْعِهْنِ ٱلْمَنفُوشِ ٥

"It is a Day whereon mankind
will be like moths scattered about.
And the mountains will be
like carded wool."
(Al-Qari'ah:4-5)

What do you know about the
Day of Qiyamah?

Allah ﷻ told us that
everything will end one day.
That is the Day of *Qiyamah*.
It is the Last Day.

Then Allah ﷻ will make us
live again.
This is called the *Akhirah*.
It is the Next Life.

No one knows how the world will look like in the *Akhirah*. Only Allah ﷻ knows. We ask Allah ﷻ to help us in this life and in the next life.

We say this *Du'a*:

رَبَّنَآ ءَاتِنَا فِى ٱلدُّنْيَا حَسَنَةً وَفِى ٱلْأَخِرَةِ حَسَنَةً وَقِنَا عَذَابَ ٱلنَّارِ

"O our Lord, give us good in this world
and good in the *Akhirah*
and save us from the pain of the fire of Hell."

WE HAVE LEARNED

☾ **Everyone will live again in *Akhirah*.**
☾ **Allah ﷻ will reward us for our good work.**

DO YOU KNOW THESE WORDS?

☾ *Akhirah, Qiyamah,* reward, pain

Link to Workbook Lesson 13

LESSON 13: THE LAST DAY AND THE NEXT LIFE

OUR DUTIES

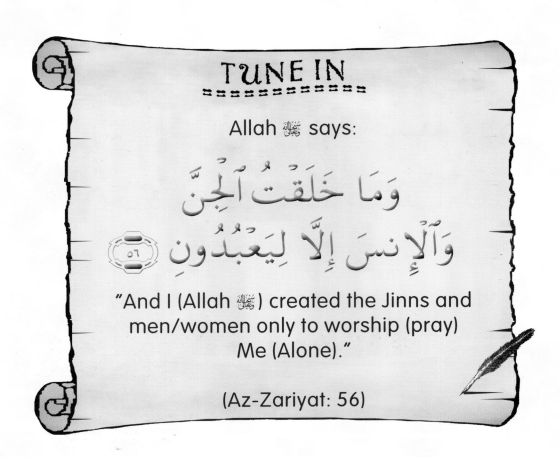

TUNE IN

Allah ﷻ says:

وَمَا خَلَقْتُ ٱلْجِنَّ وَٱلْإِنسَ إِلَّا لِيَعْبُدُونِ ۝

"And I (Allah ﷻ) created the Jinns and men/women only to worship (pray) Me (Alone)."

(Az-Zariyat: 56)

We are Muslims.
Islam is our Religion.

Allah ﷻ is our God.
We pray only to Him.

Prophet Muhammad ﷺ is our Prophet.

We do what Prophet Muhammad ﷺ told us to do.
We are Muslims.
We say the *Shahadah*.

We are Muslims.
We pray five times a day.

We are Muslims.
We fast in the
month of *Ramadan*.

We are Muslims.
We give *Zakah.*
We share our money
with the poor.

We are Muslims.
We go for *Hajj* in Makkah.

We do all of this to make Allah ﷻ happy.
These are the FIVE Pillars of Islam.
We do all of them because we LOVE Allah ﷻ.

Let us read about the Five Pillars of Islam.

WE HAVE LEARNED

☾ **We are Muslims.**
☾ **We have five duties to Allah** ﷻ
☾ **They are:** *Shahadah,* **Pray, Fast,** *Zakah* **and** *Hajj.*
☾ **We love Allah** ﷻ **.**

DO YOU KNOW THESE WORDS?

☾ **Month, believe, pillars, religion**

Link to Workbook Lesson 14

LESSON 14: OUR DUTIES

WE PRAY

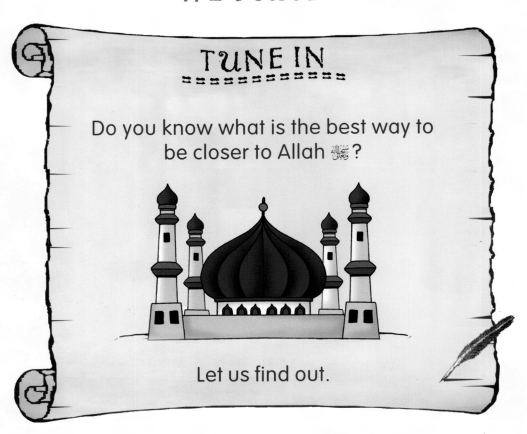

TUNE IN

Do you know what is the best way to be closer to Allah ﷻ?

Let us find out.

We are Muslims.
We pray only to Allah ﷻ.

Muslims pray to Allah ﷻ five times a day.
Prayer makes us closer to Allah ﷻ.

We pray five times every day.
Our prayer is called *Salah.*

We pray early in the morning.

This is *Fajr Salah.*
before the sun comes up.

We pray in the early
afternoon.
This is *Zuhr Salah.*

We pray in the late afternoon.
This is 'Asr Salah.

We pray again after
the sun sets.
This is Maghrib Salah.

We pray one more time
before we go to bed.
This is 'Isha Salah.

We pray early in the morning, early afternoon, and late afternoon.
We pray in the evening and night.
We pray to Allah ﷾ all the time.

We are Muslims. *Alhamdu Lillah!*

WE HAVE LEARNED

☾ **Our prayer is called *Salah*.**
☾ **We pray five times a day every day.**
☾ **The five prayers are called: *Fajr, Zuhr, 'Asr, Maghrib* and *'Isha*.**

DO YOU KNOW THESE WORDS?

☾ ***Salah, Fajr, Zuhr, 'Asr, Maghrib, 'Isha***

Link to Workbook Lesson 15

LESSON 15: WE PRAY

We pray to Allah ﷻ five times a day.
We pray on time and make Allah ﷻ happy.

Name all the prayers we do in a day.

Night

_____

Sun set

_____

Late afternoon

_____

Early afternoon

_____

Early Morning

_____

___Fajr___

Begin here

MAKING *WUDU'*

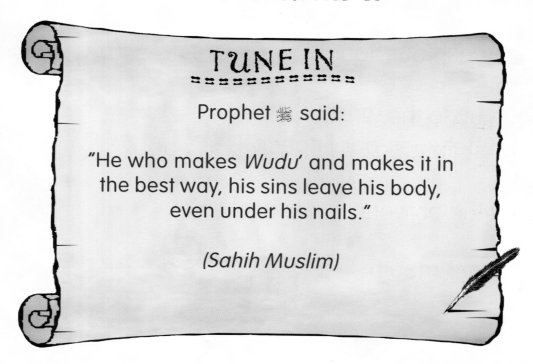

TUNE IN

Prophet ﷺ said:

"He who makes Wudu' and makes it in the best way, his sins leave his body, even under his nails."

(Sahih Muslim)

We make *Wudu'* before we pray.
We make *Wudu'* with clean water.

We begin with the *Niyyah*.
Niyyah means when we plan to do something.
We say this *Du'a* to make the *Niyyah*:

نَوَيْتُ أَنْ أَتَوَضَّأَ لِلصَّلَاةِ

"I have the intention to make *Wudu'* for *Salah*."

We say *"Bismillah ir-Rahman ir-Rahim"*.

Then we wash our hands
three times.
We wash up to the wrist.
We wash between our fingers.

We wash our mouth
three times.

We wash inside our nose
three times.

We wash our face three times.
We wash from the forehead
to the chin.

LESSON 16: MAKING *WUDU'*

We wash our right arm
and elbow three times.

Then we wash our left arm
and elbow three times.

We wipe our head and hair
with wet hands.

We wipe our ears and neck
with wet hands.

We wash our right foot and ankle.
We wash our left foot and ankle.

LESSON 16: MAKING *WUDU'*

At the end we say this *Du'a:*

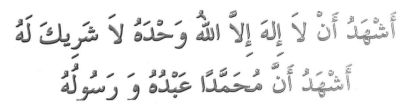

أَشْهَدُ أَنْ لاَ إِلَهَ إِلاَّ اللهُ وَحْدَهُ لاَ شَرِيكَ لَهُ
أَشْهَدُ أَنَّ مُحَمَّدًا عَبْدُهُ وَ رَسُولُهُ

" I give witness that there is no god but Allah. He does not have any partner. And I give witness that Muhammad is His Servant and Messenger."

This is how we make *Wudu'.*
We make *Wudu'* before *Salah.*

WE HAVE LEARNED

☽ We must do *Wudu'* before *Salah.*
☽ We begin our *Wudu'* with *Niyyah.*
☽ We end our *Wudu'* with *Du'a.*

DO YOU KNOW THESE WORDS?

☽ *Niyyah,* wrist, forehead, chin, ankle, witness

Link to Workbook Lesson 16

ADAB OF SALAH

TUNE IN

THE BLESSED PRAYER

Let us pray to Allah ﷺ in a *Jama'ah*
Let us strengthen our row;
To *Imam* we follow
Let us be silent
In the congregation and be respectful
To those who pray
At all times of the day.

We pray to Allah ﷺ
We follow *Adab* of *Salah*.

We stand still.
We look down.

Muslims try to pray together.
Muslims try to pray in *Jama'ah*.
Jama'ah means 'together'.
Praying in *Jama'ah*
brings us together.

We should follow the rules
of praying in *Jama'ah.*

We should stand in a line.
We should not talk.

We should stand still.
We should look down.
We should follow the *Imam.*

Let us ask Allah to help us do our *Salah.*

WE HAVE LEARNED

☾ **We should follow the Adab of Salah.**
☾ **We follow the Imam when we do Salah in Jama'ah.**

DO YOU KNOW THESE WORDS?

☾ ***Jama'ah, Imam, follow, straight line***

Link to
Workbook
Lesson 17

LESSON 17: *ADAB* OF *SALAH*

PLACES WE CAN PRAY

TUNE IN

"Tell me where I can pray?"

Can you tell Ahmad where to pray?

Allah  told Muslims to pray five times a day.
We pray at the right time.
We pray wherever we are.
We pray in clean places.
We do not pray in dirty places.

We can pray in our clean houses.

We can pray in our clean classroom.

We can pray when we travel.

We can pray in a train.
We can sit down and pray.

LESSON 18: PLACES WE CAN PRAY

We can pray in a car.
We can pray with our
seat belts on.

We can pray in a plane.

We can pray on a ship
or on a boat.

LESSON 18: PLACES WE CAN PRAY

But the best place to pray is a *Masjid*.
We pray to Allah ﷻ to help us always pray on time.

WE HAVE LEARNED

☾ **We do our prayers at a clean place.**
☾ **We can pray wherever we are.**
☾ **The best place to pray is a *Masjid*.**

DO YOU KNOW THESE WORDS?

☾ **Clean, school, travel, train, plane,**

Link to Workbook Lesson 18

WE FAST

TUNE IN

Prophet Muhammad ﷺ said:
"The *Sawm is a* shield
(against all wrong doings)".

(Al-Nisa' and Al-Tirmizi)

Do you know what is *Sawm*?

Muslims fast in the month of *Ramadan*.
We fast from *Fajr* to *Maghrib*.
We fast everyday in *Ramadan*.
We do not eat or drink when we fast.

Fasting is called *Sawm*.

We begin to fast
after we see the
moon of *Ramadan*.

We fast for 29 or 30 days.

We fast until we see
the moon of S*hawwal*.
Then we stop fasting.

We thank Allah ﷻ for blessing us with *Ramadan*.

Every Muslim fasts in *Ramadan* except:

Little Children,

Old people,

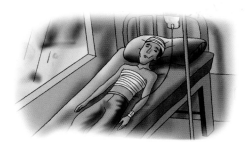

Sick people,

A person who is traveling,

A mommy who has a baby.

We respect people who fast.
We do not eat or drink in front of fasting people.
We take care of each other in *Ramadan*.

We always take care of each other.

WE HAVE LEARNED

☾ **Fasting is one of the Five Pillars of Islam.**
☾ **Muslims fast in the month of *Ramadan*.**
☾ **Muslims fast from *Fajr* to *Maghrib*.**

DO YOU KNOW THESE WORDS?

☾ ***Sawm, fasting,* sick, old, respect**

Link to Workbook Lesson 19

A SPECIAL MONTH

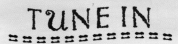

TUNE IN

Allah ﷻ has said that *Ramadan*
is the month in which
He had sent the Qur'an.
Qur'an shows the right way to every one.

Let us find out more about *Ramadan*.

Ramadan is a special month.
It is the ninth month of the
Islamic Calendar.

Allah ﷻ has blessed the
month of *Ramadan*.
It is the month of the Qur'an.
Allah ﷻ sent the Qur'an in
Ramadan.

We read the Qur'an many times a day in *Ramadan*.

Ramadan is the month of prayers.
We pray to Allah ﷾.

We pray five times every day.

We pray *Tarawih* prayers at night.
Tarawih are special prayers.
We like to go to the *Masjid* at night.

LESSON 20: A SPECIAL MONTH

Ramadan is a month of sharing.
We share with every one.

We help everyone.
We take care of each other.
We do not hurt anyone.
We do not waste our time.

We visit our friends and family.
We break our fast together.
It is called *Iftar*.
We should eat healthy food for *Iftar*.

LESSON 20: A SPECIAL MONTH

We love *Ramadan*. We feel good. We love to make Allah ﷻ happy. We do good deeds and thank Allah ﷻ.

We are Muslims *"Alhamdu Lillah"*.

WE HAVE LEARNED

- ☾ *Ramadan* is a special month.
- ☾ The Qur'an was sent in *Ramadan*.
- ☾ *Ramadan* is a month of sharing and prayers.

DO YOU KNOW THESE WORDS?

- ☾ Calendar, feel, *Tarawih*

Link to Workbook Lesson 20

THINK ABOUT IT

Muslims celebrate a special month every year.
Share what you know about this special month in the chart below.

Ramadan Is A Special Month

In which month of the Islamic calendar is *Ramadan* celebrated? ▶ _____

Ramadan is the month of… ▶ _____

What is the special prayer called? ▶ _____

What good deeds can I do in *Ramadan*? ▶ _____

Why do I like this month?

[ ]

LESSON 21

EIDUL FITR

TUNE IN

Oh look, there is a crescent!
Ramadan has sadly gone
Come my friends visit us
Time for feasting has come.

How do you feel when the
Eidul Fitr comes ?

Muslims fast in *Ramadan*.
Allah ﷻ helps us fast,
Alhamdu Lillah.

We celebrate after fasting.
We celebrate on the first of
Shawwal.

We celebrate this day
called *Eidul Fitr*.

We pray together in the *Masjid* on
Eidul Fitr.

We visit each other on *Eidul Fitr*.
This is called *Ziarah*.
We exchange gifts.

We share our food.
We give some money to the poor.
This is called *Sadaqah*.

Prophet Muhammad ﷺ said,
"Show kindness to others and
you will receive kindness."

WE HAVE LEARNED

☾ *Eidul Fitr* is a celebration after fasting.
☾ It is a time for visiting friends, neighbors and relatives and give *Sadaqah*.

DO YOU KNOW THESE WORDS?

☾ **Celebrate, share, *Ziarah*, *Sadaqah***

Link to Workbook Lesson 21

LESSON 21: *EIDUL FITR*

ALLAH ﷾ GIVES US MONEY

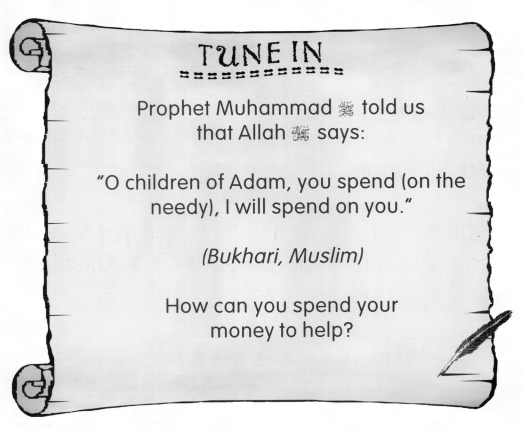

TUNE IN

Prophet Muhammad ﷺ told us that Allah ﷾ says:

"O children of Adam, you spend (on the needy), I will spend on you."

(Bukhari, Muslim)

How can you spend your money to help?

Allah ﷾ gives us money.
How does Allah ﷾ give us money?

He gave us a brain
to think.

He lets us learn how
to do things.

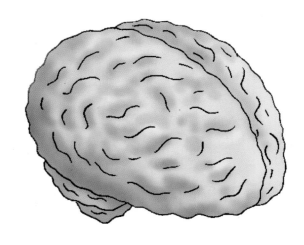

He gave us eyes to see.
He gave us mouths to speak
with.

He gave us hands and
feet to work.

He gave us good health.
We use what Allah ﷻ gave us to work.

LESSON 22: ALLAH ﷻ GIVES US MONEY

We can do different kinds of work.

We can teach.
We can work as teachers.

We can write.
We can work as writers.

We can build.
We can work as builders.

LESSON 22: ALLAH ﷻ GIVES US MONEY

We can buy and sell.
We can work in business.

We do the best work we can.
We can get money for the work
we do.

We thank Allah ﷻ for giving us
money.

We share our money with the poor.

WE HAVE LEARNED

☾ **Allah ﷻ gives us good health.**
☾ **People do different kinds of work.**
☾ **We share the money with the poor.**

DO YOU KNOW THESE WORDS?

☾ **Brain, money, teach, business, builder**

Link to
Workbook
Lesson 22

ZAKAH

TUNE IN

Allah ﷻ says in the Qur'an

فَأَقِيمُواْ ٱلصَّلَوٰةَ وَءَاتُواْ ٱلزَّكَوٰةَ وَٱعۡتَصِمُواْ

بِٱللَّهِ هُوَ مَوۡلَىٰكُمۡ

"So offer the *Salah*
and pay the *Zakah*,
and hold fast to Allah ﷻ;
He is your Master"

(Al-Hajj: 78)

Let's find out what we do with
our money.

Allah ﷻ gives people money.
He gives a lot of money to some people.
They can buy what they need.
They have extra money too.

Allah ﷻ gives less money to some people.
They can buy what they need.
Sometimes they have extra money.

Allah ﷻ gives some people very little money.

They do not have enough money.
They cannot buy what they need.

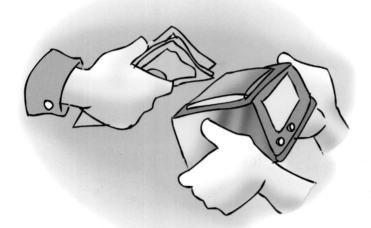

Allah ﷻ told us to share with others.

Allah ﷻ told us to share some of our money.

We share with people who do not have much.
This sharing is called *ZAKAH*.

We share with children
who do not have a mother
or father.

We share it with poor women.
We share with sick people.

Allah ﷻ wants us to share our money.
Allah ﷻ wants us to help people get what they need.

Allah ﷻ loves us when we give *ZAKAH*.

WE HAVE LEARNED

☾ **Some people make a lot of money.**
☾ **Some people do not have any money.**
☾ **We share our money with the poor.**
☾ **We pay *ZAKAH*.**

DO YOU KNOW THESE WORDS?

☾ *Zakah,* **orphans, work, little**

Link to
Workbook
Lesson 23

LESSON 23: *ZAKAH*

Allah ﷻ loves those who share.
Jameelah wants to share with others.
She can give her things.
She can give her money.
She can make things and give them too.

Think what are the things she can give to the groups of people below.

Sharing with others...

Poor children who do not have any money and new clothes for *Eid*	▶	
Some homeless people	▶	
People living in a city which had a big earthquake or tsunami	▶	

LESSON 23: *ZAKAH*

HAJJ TO MAKKAH

TUNE IN

The month of *Hajj* is here again!
Together we go,
To the House of Allah.
For we love Him
And His Messenger, Rasulullah ﷺ
For only Allah's ﷻ blessings we seek
Who helps all – strong and weak.

Let's find out more about *Hajj*.

The Ka'bah is the House of Allah.
It is in the city of Makkah.

Allah ﷻ told us to go to His House.
He told us to go to the Ka'bah for *Hajj*.
He told us to go for *Hajj* once in our lives.

Muslims go for *Hajj* in the month of *Zulhijjah*.
It is the 12th month of the Islamic Calendar.

LESSON 24: *HAJJ TO MAKKAH*

We can go for *Hajj* if we are not sick.

We can go for *Hajj* if we have enough money.

People come from all over the world to Makkah.
People come for *Hajj*.

People come by ship.

People come by plane.

People come by car and bus.

They love Allah ﷾.
They love Prophet Muhammad ﷺ.
May Allah ﷾ bless those who go
for *Hajj*.

WE HAVE LEARNED

☾ **Allah ﷾ has told Muslims to go to**
Hajj **once in our life time.**
☾ ***Hajj* is in the month of *Zulhijjah*.**
☾ **Muslims go to Makkah for *Hajj*.**

DO YOU KNOW THESE WORDS?

☾ **City, calendar, plane, ship, world**

Link to Workbook Lesson 24

LESSON 24: *HAJJ TO MAKKAH*

GETTING READY FOR *HAJJ*

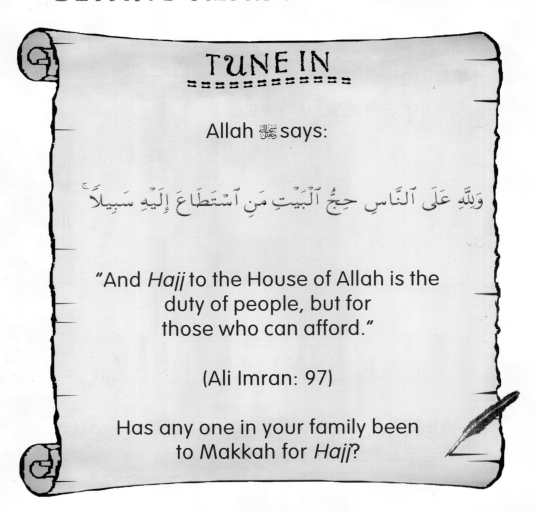

Allah ﷻ says:

وَلِلَّهِ عَلَى ٱلنَّاسِ حِجُّ ٱلْبَيْتِ مَنِ ٱسْتَطَاعَ إِلَيْهِ سَبِيلًا

"And *Hajj* to the House of Allah is the
duty of people, but for
those who can afford."

(Ali Imran: 97)

Has any one in your family been
to Makkah for *Hajj*?

Allah ﷻ told us to go to the
Ka'bah for *Hajj*.
We must get ready for *Hajj*.
We must be clean when we go
for *Hajj*.

We take a shower
before we go to Makkah.

We make *Wudu'*. We dry ourselves with a towel.

We put on special clothes.
They are called *Ihram.*

Men wear two white sheets
or large white towels.

This is the *Ihram* for men.

Women wear clean, long
clothes and cover their
heads with a large cloth.
This is the *Ihram* for women.

LESSON 25: GETTING READY FOR *HAJJ*

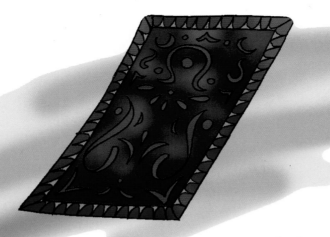

We pray two *raka'ats Salah*.
We remind ourselves that
we are going for *Hajj*.

We make *Niyyah* for *Hajj*.
Then we leave for Makkah.

All the way we say the *Talbiyah*.
"Labbaika Allahumma Labbaik!"

"I am here O Allah, I am here."

We go for *Hajj*, to pray to Allah ﷻ.
We go for *Hajj*, to thank Allah ﷻ.
We go for *Hajj*, to praise Allah ﷻ.
We love Allah ﷻ. We love Prophet Muhammad ﷺ.

WE HAVE LEARNED

☾ **We must be clean before we go for *Hajj*.**
☾ **We put on the *Ihram*.**
☾ **We say the *Talbiyah*.**

DO YOU KNOW THESE WORDS?

☾ ***Ihram*, *Talbiyah*, special, remind, ready**

Link to Workbook Lesson 25

LESSON 25: GETTING READY FOR *HAJJ*

Your family and you are getting ready to go to Makkah for *Hajj*. Complete the chart in the order of actions you need to do before you leave for *Hajj*.

First Act

We take our shower.

Second Act

Third Act

Fourth Act

Finally

We make *Niyyah* for *Hajj* and leave for Makkah.

LESSON 25: GETTING READY FOR *HAJJ*

HALAL AND HARAM

TUNE IN

Allah ﷻ says,
"O people! Eat of what is on earth,
lawful (halal) and good."

(Al-Baqarah:168)

Can you name some halal food?

Allah ﷻ gives us food to eat.
He gives us water to drink.
Allah ﷻ is the Provider.

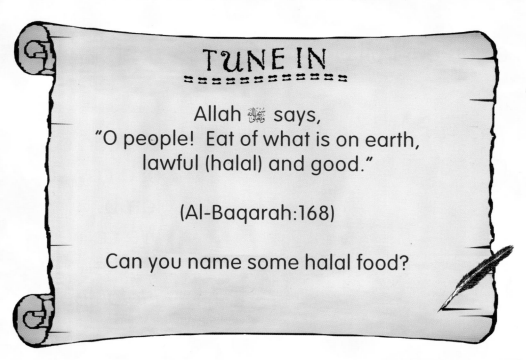

The food that Allah ﷻ
wants us to eat is *Halal.*
We must always eat
healthy and *Halal* food.
Halal food is good for us.

The food Allah ﷻ does not want us to eat is *Haram.*
We should never eat *Haram* food.
Haram food is not good for us.

We can eat
vegetables.
We can eat fruits.

We can eat the meat
of a cow, a goat or a
lamb.
We can eat fish and
chicken. These are
Halal foods.

WE HAVE LEARNED

- ☽ **Muslims eat only *Halal* food.**
- ☽ **We cannot eat food that is *Haram*.**
- ☽ ***Halal* food is good for our body.**

DO YOU KNOW THESE WORDS?

- ☽ **Food, healthy, *Halal*, *Haram*, meat, fruits**

Link to Workbook Lesson 26

HOW MUCH DO WE EAT?

TUNE IN

Mommy, daddy
Do hurry and sit
Recite the Du'a
Let us begin
To seek His blessings
Before we eat.

How much should we eat?

Muslims eat good food.
We eat healthy food.
We eat to grow.
We eat to stay healthy.

Rasulullah ﷺ taught us how to eat.
We do not eat a lot. We do not eat too little.
We eat enough to fill part of our stomach.

We stop eating before we become too full.

LESSON 27: HOW MUCH DO WE EAT?

We will feel good.
We will not feel sick.
We will have energy
to do our work.

Before we eat we say,
"*Bismillah ir-Rahman ir-Rahim*".
We say, "In the Name of Allah".

Then we say this *Du'a:*

اَللَّهُمَّ بَارِكْ لَنَا فِيمَا رَزَقْتَنَا

وَقِنَا عَذَابَ النَّارِ

**"Oh Allah bless us with the food and drink and save us
from the hell fire."**

LESSON 27: HOW MUCH DO WE EAT?

After eating we say, "Alhamdu Lillah".
We say, "All Praise is for Allah".
Then we say this *Du'a:*

الْحَمْدُ اللّهِ الَّذِي أَطْعَمَنَا
وَ سَقَانَا وَجَعَلَنَا مِنَ الْمُسْلِمِينَ

"We thank Allah who has given us to eat and to drink and has made us Muslims."

WE HAVE LEARNED

- ☾ **Muslims eat good food.**
- ☾ **We stop eating before we are full.**
- ☾ **Before eating, we say "Bismillah ir-Rahman ir-Rahim".**
- ☾ **After eating, we say "Alhamdu Lillah".**

DO YOU KNOW THESE WORDS?

- ☾ **Food, enough, energy, full, fill, part**

Link to Workbook Lesson 27

LESSON 27: HOW MUCH DO WE EAT?

ISMAIL AND HIS FAMILY

TUNE IN

Abid   Zainab

Ismail   Isra   Isa

This is Ismail's family tree.
How about yours?
Let us read about Ismail and his family.

This is Ismail.    This is his sister, Isra.

This is his brother, Isa.

Abid is his father.
Zainab is his mother.
They are his parents.

Ismail lives with his
family.
Ismail, Isra and
Isa love their parents.

They listen to their parents.
They make their parents happy.
They make Allah ﷻ happy.

Allah ﷻ says,
"*Be kind to your parents.*"

Ismail, Isra and Isa also love their grandparents.
They take care of their grandparents.
May Allah ﷻ bless Ismail's family.

WE HAVE LEARNED

☾ **Allah ﷻ loves those who are good to their parents and grandparents.**
☾ **We love and care for them.**

DO YOU KNOW THESE WORDS?

☾ **Parents, grandparents, family, care, love, listen**

Link to Workbook Lesson 28

THINK ABOUT IT

People in the family do things together. They do things that make everyone happy. Write what are the things you like to do to make your family happy.

Things I like to do to make my family happy...
a.
b.
c.
d.

Effects

It makes me proud to see my family happy.

LESSON 28: ISMAIL AND HIS FAMILY

ISMAIL AND HIS FRIENDS

TUNE IN

BEST FRIENDS

Friends are people who care.
They show you how to share.
They help when you are down.
They never make you a clown.

But the best friends of all.
Hold you when you fall
And would gently remind
That Allah ﷻ is All Kind.

Who do you think will make a
good friend?

This is Ahmad.
He is Ismail's friend.

They live next to each other.
They are neighbours.
They go to the same school.
They are best friends.

They play together.
They share their toys.
They take turns to play.

They read together. They go to *Masjid* together. They take care of each other.

We thank Allah ﷻ for our friends.

WE HAVE LEARNED

☾ **Friends care and share.**
☾ **We thank Allah ﷻ for our friends and neighbors.**

DO YOU KNOW THESE WORDS?

☾ **Friends, neighbors, read, share, take turns**

Link to Workbook Lesson 29

LESSON 29: ISMAIL AND HIS FRIENDS

BE PATIENT, ISMAIL

Fellow brothers and sisters
With whom we share
Show how much we love them
With patience and care.

How can you show someone that you
care about them and love them?

Ramadan is almost over.
Isra and Ismail kept their
fast.

They liked to do *Iftar* with
their family.

Isa wanted to fast also.
But mother told him that
he was too young to fast.

Mommy is getting ready for *Eid*.

Isra and Ismail have made a secret wish list of all the things they want for *Eid*.

Ismail really wants to have a pet for his present.
He wishes he could have a white Persian cat.

He loves cats.
Isra told mother about Ismail's wish.
Mommy said, " Ismail you have to wait. We need to ask Daddy if you can have a cat".

Ismail waited for Daddy to come home from work early for two days.
But Daddy got late.
Ismail was patient.
He waited. On Friday Daddy came home early.

LESSON 30: BE PATIENT, ISMAIL

He said, "Of course Ismail can have his cat."

It was only one week for *Eid*.

Daddy, Mommy, Isra, Ismail and Isa went for Eid shopping.

Isra got all her gifts.
Isa got his special games and Curious George books.

They went to the pet shop for Ismail's cat.
No white Persian cat.

The shopkeeper said that he will get it in two days.

Ismail had to wait. He had to be patient.

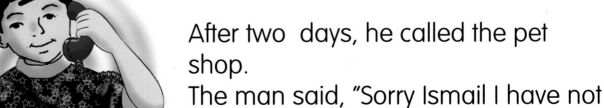

After two days, he called the pet shop.
The man said, "Sorry Ismail I have not found your cat yet."

LESSON 30: BE PATIENT, ISMAIL

Mommy said,
"Ismaill, may be you can have another pet."

"No mommy I will wait for my cat.
I will pray to Allah ﷻ to get me one."

It was the last day of *Ramadan*.
Tomorrow is *Eid*.

Mommy had wrapped all the gifts for
Isra and Isa.

But Ismail was still waiting. He was patient.

It was almost time for *Iftar*. They all sat at the dining room table to break the fast.

The door bell rang. Ismail ran to the door.

LESSON 30: BE PATIENT, ISMAIL

There at the door was Mr. James, the pet shop owner.
"*Eid Mubarak* Ismail" he said with a smile.
Here is some one special for you.

Ismail took the big gift box.
Isra and Isa wanted to see what was inside.

Ismail opened the box.
Inside was a white Persian kitten.

The kitten jumped in Ismail's hands.

LESSON 30: BE PATIENT, ISMAIL

Ismail held the kitten and ran outside to thank Mr. James.
He gave a big hug and said thank you to his parents.

This was his best *Eid* gift.
He got his wish.

WE HAVE LEARNED

- We should be patient.
- Allah ﷻ likes it when we are patient.
- Allah ﷻ helps those who are patient.

DO YOU KNOW THESE WORDS?

- **Patient, jumped, kitten, Persian**

Link to Workbook Lesson 30

LESSON 30: BE PATIENT, ISMAIL